In Loving Memory Of: